Cast Iron Cookbook 2021

Most Wanted Amazing Recipes For Cast Iron Cooking

Steven Woods

Table of Contents

ELECTRIC SMOKER BREAKFAST

1. Electric smoker Smoked Buffalo Shrimp

Preparation Time: 5 minutes

Cooking Time: 5 Minutes

Servings: 6

Ingredients:

- 1 lb. raw shrimps peeled and deveined
- 1/2 tbsp. salt
- 1/4 tbsp. garlic salt
- 1/4 tbsp. garlic powder
- 1/4 tbsp. onion powder
- 1/2 cup buffalo sauce

Directions:

1. Preheat the electric smoker grill to 450°F.
2. Coat the shrimp with both salts, garlic and onion powders.
3. Place the shrimp in a grill and cook for 3 minutes on each side.
4. Remove from the grill and toss in buffalo sauce. Serve with cheese, celery and napkins. Enjoy.

Nutrition: Calories 57, Total fat 1g, Saturated fat 0g, Total Carbs 1g, Net Carbs 1g, Protein 10g, Sugar 0g, Fiber 0g, Sodium: 1106mg, Potassium 469mg.

2. Electric smoker Teriyaki Smoked Shrimp

Preparation Time: 5 minutes

Cooking Time: 10 Minutes

Servings: 6

Ingredients:

- 1 lb. tail-on shrimp, uncooked
- 1/2 tbsp. onion powder
- 1/2 tbsp. salt
- 1/2 tbsp. Garlic powder
- 4 tbsp. Teriyaki sauce
- 4 tbsp. sriracha mayo
- 2 tbsp. green onion, minced

Directions:

1. Peel the shrimps leaving the tails then wash them removing any vein left over. Drain and pat with a paper towel to drain.
2. Preheat the electric smoker to 450°F
3. Season the shrimp with onion, salt, and garlic then place it on the grill to cook for 5 minutes on each side.
4. Remove the shrimp from the grill and toss it with teriyaki sauce. Serve garnished with mayo and onions. Enjoy.

Nutrition: Calories 87, Total fat 0g, Saturated fat 0g, Total Carbs 2g, Net Carbs 2g, Protein 16g, Sugar 1g, Fiber 0g, Sodium: 1241mg

3. Bacon-wrapped Shrimp

Preparation Time: 5 minutes

Cooking Time: 10 Minutes

Servings; 6

Ingredients:

- 1 lb. raw shrimp
- 1/2 tbsp. salt
- 1/4 tbsp. garlic powder
- 1 lb. bacon, cut into halves

Directions:

1. Preheat your smoker grill to 350F.
2. Remove the shells and tails from the shrimp then pat them dry with the paper towels.
3. Sprinkle salt and garlic on the shrimp then wrap with bacon and secure with a toothpick.
4. Place the shrimps on a baking rack greased with cooking spray.
5. Cook for 10 minutes, flip and cook for another 10 minutes or until the bacon is crisp enough.
6. Remove from the and serve.

Nutrition: Calories 204, Total fat 14g, Saturated fat 5g, Total carbs 1g, Net carbs 1g Protein 18g, Sugars 0g, Fiber 0g, Sodium 939mg

ELECTRIC SMOKER LUNCH

4. <u>Baked Steelhead</u>

Preparation Time: 15 minutes

Cooking Time: 20 minutes

Servings: 4 - 6

Ingredients:

- 1 Lemon
- 2 Garlic cloves, minced
- ½ Shallot, minced
- 3 tablespoon Butter, unsalted
- Saskatchewan seasoning, blackened
- Italian Dressing
- 1 Steelhead, (a fillet)

Directions:

1. Preheat the grill to 350F with closed lid.
2. In an iron pan place the butter. Place the pan in the grill while preheating so that the butter melts. Coat the fillet with Italian dressing. Rub with Saskatchewan rub. Make sure the layer is thin.
3. Mince the garlic and shallot. Remove the pan from the grill and add the garlic and shallots.
4. Spread the mixture on the fillet. Slice the lemon into slices. Place the slice on the butter mix.
5. Place the fish on the grate. Cook 20 - 30 minutes.

Nutrition: Calories: 230 Protein: 28g Fiber: 0g Carbohydrates 2g Fat: 14g

5. <u>Fish Stew</u>

Preparation Time: 20 minutes

Cooking Time: 25 minutes

Servings: 8

Ingredients:

- 1 jar (28oz.) Crushed Tomatoes
- 2 oz. of Tomato paste
- ¼ cup of White wine
- ¼ cup of Chicken Stock
- 2 tablespoon Butter
- 2 Garlic cloves, minced
- ¼ Onion, diced
- ½ lb. Shrimp divined and cleaned
- ½ lb. of Clams
- ½ lb. of Halibut
- Parsley
- Bread

Directions:

1. Preheat the grill to 300F with closed lid.
2. Place a Dutch oven over medium heat and melt the butter.
3. Sauté the onion for 4 - 7 minutes. Add the garlic. Cook 1 more minute.
4. Add the tomato paste. Cook until the color becomes rust red. Pour the stock and wine. Cook 10 minutes. Add the tomatoes, simmer.
5. Chop the halibut and together with the other seafood add in the Dutch oven. Place it on the grill and cover with a lid.
6. Let it cook for 20 minutes.
7. Season with black pepper and salt and set aside.
8. Top with chopped parsley and serve with bread.

Nutrition: Calories: 188 Protein: 25g Carbohydrates: 7g Fiber: 2.9g Fat: 12g

ELECTRIC SMOKER DINNER

6. <u>Lamb Rack</u>

Preparation Time: 10 minutes

Cooking Time: 30 minutes

Servings: 4

Ingredients

- 8 cloves garlic
- 1 bunch fresh thyme
- 1 tablespoon salt
- 2 teaspoons olive oil
- 1 teaspoon sherry vinegar
- 2 lbs. rack of lamb

Directions:

1. Blend the garlic and thyme with salt, vinegar, and oil. Rub the mix over the rack of lamb.
2. When ready to cook, set your smoker to 450 deg and preheat.
3. Grill the lamb for 20 minutes' fat-side down. Turn and grill for ten more minutes before slicing and serving.

Nutrition: Calories 390, Total fat 35g, Saturated fat 15g, Total Carbs 0g, Net Carbs 0g, Protein 17g, Sugar 0g, Fiber 0g, Sodium: 65mg.

7. <u>Grilled Lamb Chops With Rosemary Sauce</u>

Preparation Time:15 Mins

Cooking Time 15 Mins

Servings 6-8

Ingredients

- 1/2 Cup Extra Virgin Olive Oil, Divided
- 1/4 Cup Onion Or Shalllot, Coarsely Chopped
- 2 Cloves Garlic, Coarsely Chopped
- 2 Tbsp Soy Sauce
- 2 Tbsp Balsamic Or Sherry Vinegar
- 1 Tbsp Fresh Rosemary Needles
- 2 Tsp Dijon Mustard
- 1 Tsp Worcestershire Sauce
- Freshly Ground Black Pepper, As Needed

Directions:

1. In A Small Saucepan, Sauté The Onion And Garlic In 1 Tablespoon Of Olive Oil Over Medium Heat Until Softened And Translucent. Do Not Let Brown.
2. Transfer To A Blender Jar. Add The Soy Sauce, Vinegar, Rosemary, Mustard, And Worcestershire And Blend. Season To Taste With Black Pepper.
3. Slowly Drizzle In The Remaining Olive Oil While The Machine Is Running Until The Sauce Is Emulsified. Add A Tablespoon Of Water If The Sauce Is Too Thick. Set Aside.
4. When Ready To Cook, Set Temperature To High And Preheat, Lid Closed For 15 Minutes.
5. Brush The Lamb Chops On Both Sides With Olive Oil And Season Generously With Salt And Pepper.
6. Grill Until Lamb Chops Reach An Internal Temperature Of 135 Deg For Medium-Rare, About 4 To 6 Minutes Per Side.
7. Serve With The Rosemary Sauce For Dipping. Enjoy!

Nutrition: Calories 390, Total Fat 35g, Saturated Fat 15g, Total Carbs 0g, Net Carbs 0g, Protein 17g, Sugar 0g, Fiber 0g, Sodium: 65mg.

8. <u>Grilled Lamb Burgers With Pickled Onions</u>

Preparation Time 10 Mins

Cooking Time 10 Mins

Servings 4-6

Ingredients

- Pickled Onions
- 1/2 Red Onion, Thinly Sliced
- 6 Tbsp Lime Juice
- 1/2 Tsp Kosher Salt
- 1/2 Tsp Raw Cane Sugar
- Yogurt Sauce
- 1 Cup Greek Yogurt
- 2 Tbsp Lemon Juice
- 1 Garlic Clove, Minced
- 2 Tbsp Finely Chopped Herbs, Such As Mint, Dill And Parsley
- 1/2 Tsp Kosher Salt
- Lamb Burgers
- 1 Tbsp Olive Oil
- 1/2 Red Onion, Finely Diced
- 1 Lb Ground Lamb
- 8 Oz Ground Pork
- 3 Tbsp Finely Chopped Mint
- 2 Tbsp Finely Chopped Dill
- 3 Tbsp Finely Chopped Parsley
- 4 Garlic Cloves, Minced
- 1 1/2 Tsp Ground Cumin
- 1 Tsp Ground Coriander
- 1 Tsp Kosher Salt
- 1/2 Tsp Freshly Ground Black Pepper
- 1 Sliced Tomato
- 6 Buns
- Sliced Cucumber
- Butter Lettuce

Directions:

1. To Pickle The Onions: Place The Onion, Lime Juice, Salt And Sugar In A Small Bowl. Stir To Combine, Cover And Let Sit At Room Temperature For About 2 Hours To Soften. Refrigerate Until Ready To Use.
2. To Make The Yogurt Sauce: In A Small Bowl, Stir Together The Yogurt, Lemon Juice, Garlic, Herbs, And 1/2 Tsp Salt. Adjust The Salt To Taste. Cover And Refrigerate Until Ready To Serve, Or For Up To 2 Days.
3. To Make The Lamb Burgers: In A Small Skillet Over Medium Heat, Warm The Olive Oil. Add The Onion And Cook, Stirring Frequently Until Softened, About 7 Minutes. Transfer To A Small Plate To Cool.
4. In A Large Bowl, Combine The Lamb, Pork, Mint, Dill, Parsley, Garlic, Cumin, Coriander, Salt, Pepper, And Cooled Onions. Gently Mix With Your Hands. Do Not Overwork The Meat.
5. Divide The Mixture Into 6 Equal Balls. Press Into Patties And Transfer To A Parchment-Lined Baking Sheet. If Not Cooking Immediately, Cover And Refrigerate For Up To 8 Hours.
6. When Ready To Cook, Set The Temperature To High And Preheat, Lid Closed For 15 Minutes.
7. Place The Burgers On The Grill And Cook Until Well-Browned, About 2 To 3 Minutes Per Side For Medium-Rare, Or About 5 Minutes Per Side For Well Done.
8. Transfer Burgers To A Plate To Rest For 5 Minutes Before Serving.
9. Place Burgers On Buns And Top With A Generous Dollop Of Herbed Yogurt Sauce And Some Pickled Onions.
10. Add Lettuce, Sliced Tomatoes Or Cucumbers If Desired. Serve Immediately. Enjoy!

Nutrition: Calories 390, Total Fat 35g, Saturated Fat 15g, Total Carbs 0g, Net Carbs 0g, Protein 17g, Sugar 0g, Fiber 0g, Sodium: 65mg.

ELECTRIC SMOKER SNACKS

9. Brown Sugar Glazed Smoked Acorn Squash

Preparation Time: 20 minutes

Cooking Time: 2 hours

Servings: 10

Ingredients:

- Acorn squash (2-lbs., 0.9-kg.)
- Butter – 3 tablespoons
- Brown sugar – ¼ cup
- Salt – ¼ teaspoon
- Ground cinnamon – ¼ teaspoon
- Ground ginger – ¼ teaspoon
- Ground nutmeg – ¼ teaspoon

Directions:

1. Combine brown sugar, salt, ground cinnamon, ground ginger, and ground nutmeg in a bowl then mix well. Set aside.
2. Cut the acorn squash into halves then place in a disposable aluminum pan with the cut sides on top.
3. Brush butter onto the halved acorn squash then sprinkle the brown sugar mixture over the squash. Set aside.
4. Next, plug the electric smoker then fill the hopper with the wood pellet. Turn the switch on.
5. Set the electric smoker for indirect heat then adjust the temperature to 225°F (107°C).
6. Place the acorn squash in the electric smoker and smoke for 2 hours or until tender.
7. Once it is done, remove the smoked acorn squash from the electric smoker and place on a serving dish.
8. Serve and enjoy.

Nutrition: Calories: 125 Carbs: 25g Fat: 4g Protein: 2g

ELECTRIC SMOKER DESSERTS

10.   Chocolate Chip Cookies

Preparation Time: 30 minutes

Cooking Time: 30 minutes

Servings: 8

Ingredients:

- 1 ½ cup chopped walnuts
- 1 teaspoon vanilla
- 2 cup chocolate chips
- 1 teaspoon baking soda
- 2 ½ cup plain flour
- ½ teaspoon salt
- 1 ½ stick softened butter
- 2 eggs
- 1 cup brown sugar
- ½ cup sugar

Directions:

1. Preheat your smoker, with your lid closed, until it reaches 350 degree F.
2. Mix the baking soda, salt, and flour.
3. Cream the brown sugar, sugar, and butter. Mix in the vanilla and eggs until it comes together.
4. Slowly add in the flour while continuing to beat. Once all flour has been incorporated, add in the chocolate chips and walnuts. Using a spoon, fold into batter.
5. Place an aluminum foil onto grill. In an aluminum foil, drop spoonful of dough and bake for 17 minutes.

Nutrition: Calories: 150 Carbs: 18g Fat: 5g Protein: 10g

11.   Apple Cobbler

Preparation Time: 30 minutes

Cooking Time: 1 hour 50 minutes

Servings: 8

Ingredients:

- 8 Granny Smith apples
- 1 cup sugar
- 1 stick melted butter
- 1 teaspoon cinnamon
- Pinch salt
- ½ cup brown sugar
- 2 eggs
- 2 teaspoons baking powder
- 2 cup plain flour
- 1 ½ cup sugar

Directions:

1. Peel and quarter apples, place into a bowl. Add in the cinnamon and one c. sugar. Stir well to coat and let it set for one hour.
2. Preheat your smoker, with your lid closed, until it reaches 350 degree F.
3. In a large bowl add the salt, baking powder, eggs, brown sugar, sugar, and flour. Mix until it forms crumbles.
4. Place apples into a Dutch oven. Add the crumble mixture on top and drizzle with melted butter.
5. Place on the grill and cook for 50 minutes.

Nutrition: Calories: 152 Carbs: 26g Fat: 5g Protein: 1g

BBQ BREAKFAST

12. Sweet Thai Cilantro Chili Chicken Quarters

Preparation Time: 5 Minutes

Cooking Time: 5 Minutes

Servings: 5

Ingredients:

- chicken leg quarters, lightly coated with olive oil
- cup and 1 tsp. water
- ¾ cup rice vinegar
- ½ cup white sugar
- Tbsp. freshly chopped cilantro
- Tbsp. freshly minced ginger root
- 2 tsp. freshly minced garlic
- 2 Tbsp. crushed red pepper flakes
- 2 Tbsp. ketchup
- 2 Tbsp. cornstarch
- 2 Tbsp. fresh basil chiffonade ("chiffonade" is fancy for "thinly sliced")

Directions:

1. In a medium-sized saucepan, bring 1 cup water and the vinegar to a boil over high heat.
2. Stir in sugar, cilantro, ginger, garlic, red pepper flakes, and ketchup; simmer for 5 minutes.
3. In small mixing bowl, mix together 1 teaspoon warm water and 2 tablespoons cornstarch. Use a fork for mixing this, and what you'll end up with will resemble white school glue.
4. Slowly whisk the cornstarch mixture into the simmering sauce, and continue mixing until sauce thickens. Set aside.
5. Bring the griddle to high heat. When the griddle is hot, place the chicken quarters skin side down and cook for 8 minutes.
6. At 155°F internal temperature, glaze chicken with sauce and allow to finish cooking to an internal temperature of 165°F. Plate, garnish with basil, and serve.

Nutrition: Calories: 321; Fat: 14g; Protein:12g; Fiber:8g

13.   Simple Wood Pellet Smoked Pork Ribs

Preparation Time: 15 Minutes

Cooking Time: 5 Hours

Servings: 7

Ingredients:

- Three rack baby back ribs
- 3/4 cup pork and poultry rub
- 3/4 cup Que BBQ Sauce

Directions:

1. Peel the membrane from the backside of the ribs and trim any fat.
2. Season the pork generously with the rub.
3. Set the wood pellet grill to 180°F and preheat for 15 minutes with the lid closed.
4. Place the pork ribs on the grill and smoke them for 5 hours.
5. Remove it from the grill and wrap them in a foil with the BBQ sauce.
6. Place back the pork and increase the temperature to 350°F—Cook for 45 more minutes.
7. Remove the pork from the grill and let it rest for 20 minutes before serving. Enjoy.

Nutrition: Calories 762 Total Fat 57g Saturated Fat 17g Total Carbs 23g Net Carbs 22.7g Protein 39g Sugar 18g Fiber 0.5g Sodium: 737mg Potassium 618mg

14. Roasted Pork with Balsamic Strawberry Sauce

Preparation Time: 15 Minutes
Cooking Time: 35 Minutes
Servings: 3
Ingredients:

- 2 lb. pork tenderloin
- Salt and pepper to taste
- 2 tbsp rosemary, dried
- 2 tbsp olive oil
- 12 strawberries, fresh
- 1 cup balsamic vinegar
- 4 tbsp sugar

Directions:

1. Set the wood pellet grill to 350°F and preheat for 15 minutes with a closed lid.
2. Meanwhile, rinse the pork and pat it dry—season with salt, pepper, and rosemary.
3. In an oven skillet, heat oil until smoking. Add the pork and sear on all sides until golden brown.
4. Set the skillet in the grill and cook for 20 minutes or until the meat is no longer pink and the internal temperature is 150°F.
5. Remove the pork from the grill and let rest for 10 minutes.
6. Add berries to the skillet and sear over the stovetop for a minute. Remove the strawberries from the skillet.
7. Add vinegar in the same skillet and scrape any browned bits from the skillet bottom. Bring it to boil, then reduce heat to low. Stir in sugar and cook until it has reduced by half.
8. Slice the meat and place the strawberries on top, then drizzle vinegar sauce. Enjoy.

Nutrition: Calories 244 Total Fat 9g Saturated Fat 3g Total Carbs 15g Net Carbs 13gProtein 25g Sugar 12gFiber 2g Sodium: 159mg

BBQ LUNCH

15.　Grilled Butter Basted Rib-eye

Preparation Time: 20 Minutes

Cooking Time: 20 Minutes

Servings: 4

Ingredients:

- Two rib-eye steaks, bone-in
- Salt to taste
- Pepper to taste
- 4 tbsp butter, unsalted

Directions:

1. Mix steak, salt, and pepper in a Ziplock bag. Seal the bag and mix until the beef is well coated. Make sure that the air inside the Ziplock bag will be removed as much as possible.
2. Set the wood pellet grill temperature to high with a closed lid for 15 minutes. Place a cast-iron into the grill.
3. Place the steaks on the grill's hottest spot and cook for 5 minutes with the lid closed.
4. Open the lid, then spread butter to the skillet. When it's almost melted, place the steak on the skillet with the grilled side up.
5. Cook for 5 minutes while brushing the meat with butter. Close the lid and cook until the temperature is 130°F.
6. Take away the steak from the skillet and sit for 10 minutes before enjoying with the reserved butter.

Nutrition: Calories 745 Total fat 65g Total Carbs 5g Net Carbs 5g Protein 35g

16. Wood Pellet Smoked Ribeye Steaks

Preparation Time: 15 Minutes

Cooking Time: 35 Minutes

Servings: 1

Ingredients:

- 2-inch thick ribeye steaks
- Steak rub of choice

Directions:

1. Preheat your pellet grill to low smoke.
2. Season the steak with your favorite steak rub and place it on the grill. Let it smoke for 25 minutes.
3. Take away the steak on the grill, then change the temperature to 400°F.
4. Return the steak to the grill and sear it for 5 minutes on each side.
5. Cook until the desired temperature is achieved; 125°F-rare, 145°F-Medium, and 165°F.-Well done.
6. Wrap the steak with foil and let rest for 10 minutes before serving. Enjoy.

Nutrition: Calories 225 Total fat 10.4g Total Carbs 0.2g Protein 32.5g Sodium: 63mg, Potassium 463mg

BBQ DINNER

17.   Sweet & Savory Bacon Wrapped Dates

Preparation Time: 30 minutes

Cooking Time: 30 minutes

Servings: 16

Ingredients:

- 1 lb. thick-sliced bacon, cut in half
- 1 lb. pitted dates
- 4 ounces gorgonzola cheese
- 32 toothpicks

Directions:

1. Slice dates up one side and open them up. Pinch off a piece of cheese and place it into the center of the date.
2. Close the halves of the dates and wrap a half-slice of bacon around the outside, secure with a toothpick.
3. Lay a single sheet of foil over pellet grill grates and add the wraps in a single layer.
4. Grill until bacon starts to crisp, then flip each wrap over.
5. When the second side is crisped, remove to a platter lined with paper towels, allow to cool slightly before serving.

Nutrition: Calories: 248 Carbs: 33g Fat: 10g Protein: 10g

18. Jalapeño Pepper Bombs

Preparation Time: 10 minutes

Cooking Time: 15 minutes

Servings: 10

Ingredients:

- 10 fresh jalapenos
- 20 Cheddar Little Smokies
- 8oz. Cream Cheese
- 2 lbs. Bacon (½ strip each)
- 1/8 Sweet Onion (diced)
- 1 Tbsp. Sugar

Directions:

1. Soften cream cheese and blend in sugar and onions.
2. Slice Jalapenos in half, lengthwise, and trim away all seeds and membranes, rinse.
3. Spoon 1 teaspoon of cream cheese mixture into each side. Place 1 smokie on each half and press it into the cream cheese.
4. Add the bombs in a single layer. Grill until bacon starts to crisp, moving to cool side of the grill starts flaring up, and then remove to a platter lined with paper towels.
5. Allow to cool slightly and serve.

Nutrition: Calories: 281 Carbs: 10g Fat: 24g Protein: 6g

BBQ SNACKS

19.   Tomato and Corn Salsa with Lime

Preparation time: 15 minutes

Cooking time: 15 to 20 minutes

Servings 6 to 8

Ingredients;

- 4 luscious ripe red tomatoes (about 2 pounds / 907 g), cut in half widthwise
- 4 jalapeño peppers, stemmed and cut in half lengthwise (seeded for a milder salsa; seeds left in for hotter)
- 2 ears sweet corn, shucked
- 1 small sweet onion, peeled and quartered
- ½ cup chopped fresh cilantro
- ¼ cup fresh lime juice (2 to 3 limes), or to taste
- Coarse salt (sea or kosher), to taste
- Tortilla chips, for serving

Directions:

1. Set up your smoker following the manufacturer's instructions and preheat to 225°F (107°C). Add the wood as specified by the manufacturer.
2. Place the tomatoes and jalapeños (both cut side up), corn, and onion in the smoker. Smoke the vegetables long enough to impart a smoke flavor (but not so long that you cook them), 15 to 20 minutes. Transfer the vegetables to a platter and let cool to room temperature.
3. Lay the corn flat on a cutting board and slice the kernels off the cob using broad strokes of a chef's knife. Transfer the corn kernels to a large bowl.
4. Coarsely chop the tomatoes, jalapeños, and onion by hand or in a food processor. Add to the corn and stir in the cilantro, lime juice, and salt to taste. The salsa should be highly seasoned. Transfer the salsa to a serving bowl. Serve with chips alongside.

Nutrition: Calories: 57 Total Fat: 3 g Saturated Fat: 1 g Total Carbs: 6 g Net Carbs: 4 g Protein: 4 g Sugars: 2 g Fiber: 2 g Sodium: 484 mg

GLUTEN-FREE, EGG-FREE

20. <u>Delicious Smoked Apple Pie</u>

Preparation Time: 10-15 minutes

Cooking Time: 20-30 minutes

Servings; 4

Ingredients

- 5 apples
- ¼ cup of sugar
- 1 tablespoon cornstarch
- Flour as needed
- 1 refrigerated pie crust
- ¼ cup peach preserve

Directions:

1. Take your drip pan and add water, cover with aluminum foil. Pre-heat your smoker to 275 degrees F
2. Use water fill water pan halfway through and place it over drip pan. Add wood chips to the side tray
3. Take a medium-sized bowl and add apples, sugar, cornstarch and stir well until combined thoroughly
4. Transfer to one side
5. Dust a work surface with flour and roll out your pie crust
6. Transfer pie crust into a pie pan (no greasing)
7. Spread preserve on bottom of pan and top with apple slices
8. Transfer into smoker and smoke for 30-40 minutes
9. Serve and enjoy!

Nutrition; Calories: 236 Fat: 9g Carbohydrates: 39g Protein: 2g

BBQ DESSERTS

21. <u>Wood Pellet Smoked Vegetables</u>

Preparation Time: 5 Minutes

Cooking Time: 15 Minutes

Servings: 6

Ingredients:

- 1 ear corn, fresh, husks and silk strands removed
- 1yellow squash, sliced
- 1 red onion, cut into wedges
- 1 green pepper, cut into strips
- 1 red pepper, cut into strips
- 1 yellow pepper, cut into strips
- 1 cup mushrooms, halved
- 2 tbsp oil
- 2 tbsp chicken seasoning

Directions:

1. Soak the pecan wood pellets in water for an hour. Remove the pellets from water and fill the smoker box with the wet pellets.
2. Place the smoker box under the grill and close the lid. Heat the grill on high heat for 10 minutes or until smoke starts coming out from the wood chips.
3. Meanwhile, toss the veggies in oil and seasonings then transfer them into a grill basket.
4. Grill for 10 minutes while turning occasionally. Serve and enjoy.

Nutrition: Calories 97 Total fat 5g Total Carbs 11g Protein 2g Sugar 1g Fiber 3g Sodium: 251mg Potassium 171mg

CAMPING BREAKFAST

22.   Lemon Pepper Chicken Wings

Preparation Time: 15 Minutes

Cooking Time: 45 Minutes

Servings: 4

Ingredients:

- 4 lbs. chicken wings
- 2 tsp garlic powder
- 1/4 cup ground black pepper
- 2 tsp kosher salt
- 2 tbsp lemon zest
- 2 tbsp olive oil
- 3 tsp dried thyme

Directions:

1. Preheat your pellet grill to 400°F.
2. In a bowl, mix ground pepper, lemon zest, thyme, garlic powder, and kosher salt.
3. Add wings to a separate, large bowl and then add olive oil. Toss wings until lightly coated with olive oil. Next, add a little bit of seasoning at a time and toss. Repeat until wings are seasoned to your preference.
4. Place wings on heated grill grate and cook for 30 minutes, flipping halfway through after 15 minutes.
5. Remove wings from grill after they are thoroughly cooked and crispy on the outside.
6. Allow to cool at room temperature for at least 10 minutes then enjoy!

Nutrition: Calories per serving: 430   Carbohydrates: 2.1g Protein: 25.4g Fat: 33g Sodium: 331mg Fiber: 0.7g

23.   Grilled Chicken Fajitas

Preparation Time: 30 Minutes

Cooking Time: 45 Minutes

Servings: 4

Ingredients:

- 1 lb. boneless skinless chicken breast
- 1/2 green bell pepper, julienned
- 8 tortillas, flour or corn
- 1/2 red bell pepper, julienned
- 1 avocado, sliced
- Toppings: shredded cheese, salsa,
- 1/2 cup yellow onion, julienned
- guacamole, sour cream, jalapeños

RUB INGREDIENTS

- 1 tsp kosher salt
- 1 tsp garlic powder
- 1 tsp dried oregano
- 1 tsp chili powder
- 1 tsp cumin
- 1 tsp paprika

Directions:

1. Preheat your pellet grill to 350°F.
2. Mix all rub ingredients in a small bowl.
3. Rinse chicken under water then coat the chicken with the rub mixture, and thoroughly coat the chicken breast.
4. Place chicken breast on the pellet grill and cook, flipping after about 5 minutes. Cook for about 10-12 minutes total, or until no longer pink.
5. After chicken has cooked all the way through, put out from heat and allow to rest for 10 minutes.
6. Add onions, green pepper and red pepper to a stove pan in your kitchen while the chicken rests. Add a splash of olive oil (if desired) and sauté the veggies for about 8 minutes or until they begin to soften.
7. Slice the chicken into thin strips.
8. Serve immediately on corn or flour tortillas. Add onions and avocado slices.
9. Squeeze lime wedges over the steak and add any additional toppings as desired like shredded cheese, salsa, guacamole, sour cream, etc.

Nutrition: Calories per serving: 430   Carbohydrates: 2.1g Protein: 25.4g Fat: 33g Sodium: 331mg Fiber: 0.7g

24.   Smoked Guacamole

Preparation Time: 15 Minutes

Cooking Time: 30 Minutes

Servings: 8

Ingredients:

- 1/4 cup chopped Cilantro
- 7 Avocados, peeled and seeded
- ¼ cup chopped Onion, red
- ¼ cup chopped tomato
- 3 ears corn
- 1 teaspoon of Chile Powder
- 1 teaspoon of Cumin
- 2 tablespoons of Lime juice
- 1 tablespoon minced Garlic
- 1 Chile, poblano
- Black pepper and salt to taste

Directions:

1. Preheat the grill to 180F with closed lid.
2. Smoke the avocado for 10 min.
3. Set the avocados aside and increase the temperature of the girl to high.
4. Once heated grill the corn and chili. Roast for 20 minutes.
5. Cut the corn. Set aside. Place the chili in a bowl. Cover it with a wrapper and let it sit for about 10 minutes. Peel the chili and dice. Add it to the kernels.
6. In a bowl mash the avocados, leave few chunks. Add the remaining ingredients and mix.
7. Serve right away because it is best eaten fresh. Enjoy!

Nutrition: Calories: 51 Protein: 1g Carbs: 3g Fat: 4.5g

CAMPING LUNCH

25.   Chicken Fajitas on a Wood Pellet Grill

Preparation Time: 10 minutes
Cooking Time: 40 minutes
Servings: 1
Ingredients:

- Chicken breast - 2 lbs., thin sliced
- Red bell pepper - 1 large
- Onion - 1 large
- Orange bell pepper - 1 large
- Seasoning mix
- Oil - 2 tablespoon
- Onion powder - ½ tablespoon
- Granulated garlic - ½ tablespoon
- Salt - 1 tablespoon

Directions:

1. Preheat the grill to 450 degrees.
2. Mix the seasonings and oil.
3. Add the chicken slices to the mix.
4. Line a large pan with a non-stick baking sheet.
5. Let the pan heat for 10 minutes.
6. Place the chicken, peppers, and other vegetables in the grill.
7. Grill for 10 minutes or until the chicken is cooked.
8. Remove it from the grill and serve with warm tortillas and vegetables.

Nutrition: Carbohydrates: 5 g Protein: 29 g Fat: 6 g Sodium: 360 mg Cholesterol: 77 mg

26.   Chicken Wings in Wood Pellets

Preparation Time: 10 minutes

Cooking Time: 50 minutes

Servings: 1

Ingredients:

- Chicken wings - 6-8 lbs.
- Canola oil – 1/3 cup
- Barbeque seasoning mix - 1 tablespoon

Directions:

1. Combine the seasonings and oil in one large bowl.
2. Put the chicken wings in the bowl and mix well.
3. Turn your wood pellet to the 'smoke' setting and leave it on for 4-5 minutes.
4. Set the heat to 350 degrees and leave it to preheat for 15 minutes with the lid closed.
5. Place the wings on the grill with enough space between the pieces.
6. Let it cook for 45 minutes or until the skin looks crispy.
7. Remove from the grill and serve with your choice of sides.

Nutrition: Protein: 33 g Fat: 8 g Sodium: 134 mg Cholesterol: 141 mg

CAMPING DINNER

27.   Grill Spicy Sweet Potatoes

Preparation time: 10 minutes

Cooking time: 35 minutes

Servings: 6

Ingredients:

- 2 lb. sweet potatoes, cut into chunks
- 1 red onion, chopped
- 2 tbsp oil
- 2 tbsp orange juice
- 1 tbsp roasted cinnamon
- 1 tbsp salt
- 1/4 tbsp Chipotle chili pepper

Directions:

1. Preheat the wood pellet grill to 425°F with the lid closed. Toss the sweet potatoes with onion, oil, and juice.
2. In a mixing bowl, mix cinnamon, salt, and pepper, then sprinkle the mixture over the sweet potatoes. Spread the potatoes on a lined baking dish in a single layer.
3. Place the baking dish in the grill and grill for 30 minutes or until the sweet potatoes are tender. Serve and enjoy.

Nutrition: Calories 145 fat 5g Carbs 23g Protein 2g

28. Grilled Stuffed Zucchini

Preparation time: 5 minutes

Cooking time: 11 minutes

Servings: 8

Ingredients:

- 4 zucchinis
- 5 tbsp olive oil
- 2 tbsp red onion, chopped
- 1/4 tbsp garlic, minced
- 1/2 cup bread crumbs
- 1/2 cup mozzarella cheese, shredded
- 1 tbsp fresh mint
- 1/2 tbsp salt
- 3 tbsp parmesan cheese

Directions:

1. Slice your zucchini lengthwise, then scoop out the pulp, then brush the shells with oil. In a non-stick skillet, sauté pulp, onion, and remaining oil. Add garlic and cook for a minute.
2. Put bread crumbs, then cook until golden brown. Remove from heat and stir in mozzarella cheese, fresh mint, and salt.
3. Spoon the batter into the shells and sprinkle parmesan cheese. Place in a grill, set at 350 F and grill for 10 minutes or until the zucchini is tender.

Nutrition: Calories 186 Fat 10g Carbs 17g Protein 9g

29.   Grilled Mexican Street Corn

Preparation time: 5 minutes

Cooking time: 25 minutes

Servings: 6

Ingredients:

- 6 corn on the cob, shucked
- 1 tbsp olive oil
- kosher salt and pepper to taste
- 1/4 cup mayo
- 1/4 cup sour cream
- 1 tbsp garlic paste
- 1/2 tbsp chili powder
- pinch of ground red pepper
- 1/2 cup cotija cheese, crumbled
- 1/4 cup cilantro, chopped
- 6 lime wedges

Directions:

1. Oiled the corn using olive oil and sprinkle with salt. Place the corn on a wood pellet grill set at 350°F. Cook for 25 minutes as you turn it occasionally.
2. Meanwhile, mix mayo, cream, garlic, chili, and red pepper until well combined. Let the corn rest for some minutes, then brush with the mayo mixture.
3. Sprinkle cotija cheese, more chili powder, and cilantro. Serve with lime wedges. Enjoy.

Nutrition: Calories 144 Fat 5g Carbs 10g Protein 0g

CAMPING SNACKS

30.   Spiced Tomahawk Steaks

Preparation Time: 5 minutes

Cooking Time: 1 hour

Servings: 4

Smoke Temperature: 135Farenheit

Preferred Wood Pellet: Apricot or Alder

Ingredients:

- 2 tablespoons ground black pepper
- 2 tablespoons kosher salt
- 1 tablespoon paprika
- 1/2 tablespoon brown sugar
- 1/2 tablespoon onion powder
- 1/2 tablespoon garlic powder
- 1 teaspoon ground mustard
- 1/4 teaspoon cayenne pepper
- 2 large Tomahawk steaks

Directions:

1. Stir together all the ingredients except the steaks in a small bowl. Liberally season the steaks with the rub mixture.
2. Set the Trigger and preheat, lid closed for 15 minutes.
3. Take off the steaks and set aside to rest.
4. Increase the grill temperature to 450°F (232°C). Cook the steaks each side.
5. Remove the steaks from the grill cool for 5 minutes before serving.

Nutrition: Calories: 764 Fat: 55g Carbohydrates: 2g Protein: 63g

CAMPING DESSERTS

31.   Coconut Dipping Sauce

Preparation Time: 10 Minutes

Cooking Time: 30 Minutes

Servings: 4

Ingredients:

- 4 tablespoons coconut milk
- 1 tablespoon curry paste
- 2 tablespoons lime juice
- 2 tsp soy sauce
- 1 tsp fish sauce
- 1 tsp honey

Directions:

1. In a blender place all ingredients and blend until smooth
2. Pour smoothie in a glass and serve

Nutrition: Calories: 30 Carbs: 12g Fat: 1g Protein: 0g

32.   Black Bean Dipping Sauce

Preparation Time: 10 Minutes

Cooking Time: 30 Minutes

Servings: 4

Ingredients:

- 2 tablespoons black bean paste
- 2 tablespoons peanut butter
- 1 tablespoon maple syrup
- 2 tablespoons olive oil

Directions:

1. In a blender place all ingredients and blend until smooth
2. Pour smoothie in a glass and serve

Nutrition: Calories: 20 Carbs: 13g Fat: 1g Protein: 0g

DUTCH BREAKFAST

33. Bacon and Asparagus Spears

Preparation Time: 15 Minutes

Cooking Time: 8 Minutes

Servings: 4

Ingredients:

- 20 spears asparagus
- Four bacon slices
- One tablespoon olive oil
- One tablespoon sesame oil
- One garlic clove, crushed

Directions:

1. Warm your Dutch oven to 380 degrees F
2. Take a small bowl and add oil, crushed garlic, and mix
3. Separate asparagus into four bunches and wrap them in bacon
4. Brush wraps with oil and garlic mix, transfer to your Dutch oven basket
5. Cook for 8 minutes
6. Serve and enjoy!

Nutrition: Calories: 175 Fat: 15g Carbohydrates: 6g Protein: 5g

34. Healthy Low Carb Fish Nugget

Preparation Time: 5 Minutes

Cooking Time: 10 Minutes

Servings: 4

Ingredients:

- 1-pound fresh cod
- Two tablespoons olive oil
- ½ cup almond flour
- Two larges finely beaten eggs
- 1-2 cups almond meal

Directions:

1. Preheat your Dutch oven to 388 degrees F
2. Take a food processor and add olive oil, almond meal, salt, and blend
3. Take three bowls and add almond flour, almond meal, beaten eggs individually
4. Take cods and cut them into slices of 1-inch thickness and 2-inch length
5. Dredge slices into flour, eggs, and crumbs
6. Transfer nuggets to Dutch oven cooking basket and cook for 10 minutes until golden
7. Serve and enjoy!

Nutrition: Calories: 196 Fat: 14g Carbohydrates: 6g Protein: 14g

DUTCH LUNCH

35.   <u>Beef Curry</u>

Preparation Time: 6 Minutes

Cooking Time: 44 Minutes

Servings: 4

Ingredients:

- 2 lb. beef (cut into cubes)
- 2 tbsp. tomato sauce
- 3 medium potatoes (cut into cubes)
- 2 yellow onions chopped
- 2 tbsp. olive oil
- 1 tbsp. wine mustard
- 2 garlic cloves (minced)
- 2-1/2 tbsp. curry
- 10 oz. can coconut milk
- Salt and black pepper to taste

Directions:

1. Preheat the dutch oven to 3600F.
2. Place a pan over medium heat (make sure the pan fits into your dutch oven), add oil, and heat until shimmering. Add the onions and garlic, cook for 4 minutes or until translucent. Add the beef, curry powder, tomato sauce, coconut milk, salt, and pepper.
3. Stir and transfer to the dutch oven; set the time for 40 minutes.
4. Serve and enjoy.

Nutrition: Calories: 231kcal, Fat: 15g, Carb: 20g, Proteins: 27g

36.   Garlic and Bell Pepper Beef

Preparation Time: 30 Minutes

Cooking Time: 21 Minutes

Servings: 4

Ingredients:

- 11 oz. steak fillets (sliced)
- 1/2 cup beef stock
- 2 tbsp. olive oil
- 2 tbsp. fish sauce
- 4 cloves garlic (pressed)
- 1 red pepper (cut into thin strips)
- 4 green onions (sliced)
- 1 tbsp. sugar
- 2 tsp. corn flour
- Black pepper to taste

Directions:

1. In a pan, add beef, oil, garlic, black pepper, and bell pepper, stir, cover, and keep in the refrigerator for 30 minutes.
2. Preheat the dutch oven to 3600F.
3. Put the pan to the dutch oven and cook for 14 minutes. In a bowl, mix sugar and fish sauce, pour over the beef and cook for an additional 7 minutes.
4. Serve and enjoy.

Nutrition: Calories: 243kcal, Fat: 3g, Carb: 24g, Proteins: 38g

37.   **Beef and Green Onion Marinade**

Preparation Time: 10 Minutes

Cooking Time: 20 Minutes

Servings: 4

Ingredients:

- 1 lb. lean beef
- 1 cup of soy sauce
- 5 garlic cloves (minced)
- 1/4 cup sesame seeds
- 1/2 cup of water
- 1 tsp. black pepper
- 1/4 cup brown sugar
- 1 cup green onion

Directions:

1. In a bowl, add soy sauce, onions, sugar, water, garlic, sesame seed, and pepper, whisk. Add the beef and toss to coat, leave for 10 minutes.
2. Preheat the dutch oven to 3900F, drain the beef, and transfer to the dutch oven. Cook for 20 minutes.
3. Serve with salad and enjoy.

Nutrition: Calories: 329kcal, Fat: 8g, Carb: 24g, Proteins: 22g

DUTCH DINNER

38.   **Buttered Salmon**

Preparation Time: 10 Minutes

Cooking Time: 10 Minutes

Servings: 2

Ingredients:

- 2 (6-ounce) salmon fillets
- Salt and freshly ground black pepper, to taste
- 1 tablespoon butter, melted

Directions:

1. Season each salmon fillet with salt and black pepper and then, coat with the butter.
2. Press "Power Button" of Power XL Digital Air Fry Oven and turn the dial to select "Air Fry" mode.
3. Press "Time Button" and again turn the dial to set the cooking time to 10 minutes.
4. Now push "Temp Button" and rotate the dial to set the temperature at 360 degrees F.
5. Press "Start/Pause" button to start.
6. When the unit beeps to show that it is preheated, open the lid and grease the air fry basket.
7. Arrange the salmon fillets into the prepared air fry basket and insert in the oven.
8. When cooking time is complete, open the lid and transfer the salmon fillets onto serving plates.
9. Serve hot.

Nutrition: Calories: 276 Fat: 16.3g Sat Fat: 5.2g Carbohydrates: 0g Fiber: 0g Sugar: 0g Protein: 33.1g

39. <u>Herbed Salmon</u>

Preparation Time: 10 Minutes

Cooking Time: 10 Minutes

Servings: 2

Ingredients:

- 1 tablespoon fresh lime juice
- ½ tablespoons olive oil
- Salt and freshly ground black pepper, to taste
- 1 garlic clove, minced
- ½ teaspoon fresh thyme leaves, chopped
- ½ teaspoon fresh rosemary, chopped
- 2 (7-ounce) salmon fillets

Directions:

1. In a bowl, add all the ingredients except the salmon and mix well.
2. Add the salmon fillets and coat with the mixture generously.
3. Press "Power Button" of Power XL Digital Air Fry Oven and turn the dial to select "Air Bake" mode.
4. Press "Time Button" and again turn the dial to set the cooking time to 10 minutes.
5. Now push "Temp Button" and rotate the dial to set the temperature at 400 degrees F.
6. Press "Start/Pause" button to start.
7. When the unit beeps to show that it is preheated, open the lid.
8. Arrange the salmon fillets over the greased wire rack and insert in the oven.
9. Flip the fillets once halfway through.
10. When cooking time is complete, open the lid and transfer the salmon fillets onto serving plates.
11. Serve hot.

Nutrition: Calories: 297 Fat: 15.8g Sat Fat: 2.3g Carbohydrates: 0.9g Fiber: 0.3g Sugar: 0g Protein: 38.6g

DUTCH SNACKS

40.   Delicious Taco Cups

Preparation Time: 5 to 10 Minutes

Cooking Time: 10 Minutes

Servings: 4

Ingredients:

- 1 cup cheddar cheese, shredded
- 2 tablespoons taco seasoning
- ½ cup tomatoes, chopped
- 1-pound ground beef, cooked
- 12 wonton wrappers

Directions:

1. Press wrappers firmly onto the muffin pan
2. Transfer the pan inside your Power XL Smart XL Grill
3. Air Fry on AIR CRISP mode for 5 minutes at 400 degrees F
4. Top with ground beef and tomatoes,
5. Sprinkle taco seasoning, cheese
6. Air Fry for 5 minutes more
7. Enjoy!

Nutrition: Calories: 431, Fat: 21 g, Saturated Fat: 7 g, Carbohydrates: 30 g, Fiber: 5 g, Sodium: 604 mg, Protein: 31 g

DUTCH DESSERTS

41. <u>Baked Cheese Crisps</u>

Preparation Time: 5 Minutes

Cooking Time: 15 Minutes

Servings: 4

Ingredients:

- 1/2 cup Parmesan cheese, shredded
- 1 cup Cheddar cheese, shredded
- One teaspoon Italian seasoning
- 1/2 cup marinara sauce

Directions:

1. Begin by preheating your Dutch ovenand set it to 350 degrees F. Place a piece of parchment paper in the cooking basket.
2. Mix the cheese with the Italian seasoning.
3. Add around one tablespoon of the cheese mixture (per crisp to the basket, making sure they are not touching—Bake for 6 minutes or until browned to your liking.
4. Work in batches and place them on a large tray to cool slightly. Serve with the marinara sauce. Bon appétit!

Nutrition: Calories 198 Fat 17g Carbs 7g Protein 12g Sugar 4g

42. Puerto Rican Tostones

Preparation Time: 5 Minutes

Cooking Time: 15 Minutes

Servings: 2

Ingredients:

- One ripe plantain, sliced
- One tablespoon sunflower oil
- A pinch of grated nutmeg
- A pinch of kosher salt

Directions:

1. Toss the plantains with the oil, nutmeg, and salt in a bowl.
2. Cook in the preheated Dutch ovenat 400 degrees F for 10 minutes, shaking the cooking basket halfway through the cooking time.
3. Regulate the seasonings to taste and serve immediately.

Nutrition: Calories 151 Fat 1g Carbs 29g Protein 6g Sugar 17g

CAST IRON BREAKFAST

43. Bacon Wrapped Scallops

Preparation Time: 0 minutes

Cooking Time: 30 minutes

Servings: 4

Smoke Temperature: 135Farenheit

Preferred Wood Pellet: Hickory or Apple

Ingredients:

- 12 scallops
- 12 bacon slices
- 3 tablespoons lemon juice
- Pepper to taste

Directions:

1. Turn on your wood pellet grill.
2. Set it to smoke.
3. Let it burn for 5 minutes while the lid is open.
4. Set it to 400 degrees F.
5. Wrap the scallops with bacon.
6. Secure with toothpick.
7. Pour with the lemon juice and with pepper.
8. Add the scallops to a baking tray.
9. Place the tray on the grill.
10. Grill for 20 minutes.

Nutrition: Calories: 180 Carbs: 1g Fat: 8g Protein: 10g

44. Swordfish Steaks with Corn Salsa

Preparation Time: 0 minutes

Cooking Time: 30 minutes

Servings: 4

Smoke Temperature: 135Farenheit

Preferred Wood Pellet: Hickory or Apple

Ingredients:

- 4 whole ears corn, husked
- Olive oil, as needed
- Salt and black pepper, to taste
- 1 pint cherry tomatoes
- 1 whole Serrano chili, chopped
- 1 whole red onion, diced
- 1 whole lime, juiced
- 4 whole swordfish fillets

Directions:

1. When ready to cook, set the Trigger to High and preheat, lid closed for 15 minutes.
2. Place the corn on the grill grate and grill for 12 to 15 minutes, or until cooked through and lightly browned. Set aside to cool.
3. Transfer to a medium bowl. Stir in the tomatoes, Serrano, red onion and lime juice.
4. Arrange the fillets on the grill grate and grill for about 18 minutes.
5. Serve the grilled swordfish topped with the corn salsa.

Nutrition: Calories: 87 Carbs: 10g Fat: 2g Protein: 6g

CAST IRON LUNCH

45.   Fromage Macaroni and Cheese

Preparation Time: 30 Minutes

Cooking Time: 1 Hour

Servings: 8

Ingredients:

- ¼ c. all-purpose flour
- ½ stick butter
- Butter, for greasing
- One-pound cooked elbow macaroni
- One c. grated Parmesan
- 8 ounces cream cheese
- Two c. shredded Monterey Jack
- 3 t. garlic powder
- Two t. salt
- One t. pepper
- Two c. shredded Cheddar, divided
- Three c. milk

Directions:

1. Add the butter to a pot and melt. Mix in the flour. Stir constantly for a minute. Mix in the pepper, salt, garlic powder, and milk. Let it boil.
2. After lowering the heat, let it simmer for about 5 mins, or until it has thickened. Remove from the heat.
3. Mix in the cream cheese, parmesan, Monterey Jack, and 1 ½ c. of cheddar. Stir everything until melted. Fold in the pasta.
4. Add wood pellets to your smoker and keep your cooker's startup procedure. Preheat your smoker, with your lid closed, until it reaches 225.
5. Butter a 9" x 13" baking pan. Pour the macaroni mixture into the pan and lay on the grill. Cover and allow it to smoke for an hour, or until it has become bubbly. Top the macaroni with the rest of the cheddar during the last
6. Serve.

Nutrition: Calories: 180 Carbs: 19g Fat: 8g Protein: 8g

46. Spicy Barbecue Pecans

Preparation Time: 15 Minutes

Cooking Time: 1 Hour

Servings: 2

Ingredients:

- 2 ½ t. garlic powder
- 16 ounces raw pecan halves
- One t. onion powder
- One t. pepper
- Two t. salt
- One t. dried thyme
- Butter, for greasing
- 3 T. melted butter

Directions:

1. Add wood pellets to your smoker and follow your cooker's startup method.
2. Preheat your smoker, with your lid closed, until it reaches 225.
3. Cover and smoke for an hour, flipping the nuts one. Make sure the nuts are toasted and heated. They should be removed from the grill.
4. Set aside to cool and dry.

Nutrition: Calories: 150 Carbs: 16g Fat: 9g Protein: 1g

CAST IRON DINNER

47.   Corn and Cheese Chile Relents

Preparation time: 30 minutes

Cooking time: 1 hour and 10 minutes

Servings: 12

Smoke Temperature: 135Farenheit

Preferred Wood Pellet: Apricot or Alder

Ingredients:

- 2 lbs. Ripe Tomatoes, Chopped
- 4 cloves garlic
- 1/2 cup sweet onion
- 1 jalapeno, stemmed
- 8 large Green New Mexican
- 3 ears sweet corn
- 1/2 Tsp. Dry Oregano,
- 1 Tsp. Ground
- 1 Tsp. chili powder
- 1/8 Tsp. Ground Cinnamon
- Salt and Freshly Ground Pepper
- 3 cups Grated Monterey Jack
- 1/2 cup Mexican Cream
- 1 cup quest fresco, crumbled
- Fresh Cilantro Leaves
- Intolerances:
- Gluten-Free - Egg-Free
- Lactose-Free

Directions:

1. Place the tomatoes, garlic, onion, and jalapeno in a shallow baking dish on the grill grate.
2. Start grill on Smoke with the lid open until the fire is established (4 to 5 minutes).
3. Set the temperature and preheat, lid closed, for 10 to 15 minutes.
4. Arrange the New Mexican chilies and the sweet corn on the grate and grill until the chilies are blistered and blackened in spots and the corn is lightly browned, 15 to 20 minutes for the chilies and 10 to 15 minutes for the corn, turning with tongs as needed.
5. Reduce the heat to 350°F if you intend to bake the relents right away.
6. Pour the cooled tomato mixture in a blender.

7. With a small paring knife, slit each chili lengthwise from the shoulder (just below the stem) to the tip. Pull out the seeds and set the chilies aside while you make the filling.
8. Slice the corn off the cobs
9. Gently stir in the sour cream. Season with salt and pepper. Generously stuff the chilies with the corn-cheese mixture
10. Sprinkle some of the reserved cheese.
11. Enjoy!

Nutrition: Calories: 500 Fat: 30gCholesterol: 165mg Carbs: 60g Protein: 20g

48. <u>Mashed Potatoes</u>

Preparation time: 5 minutes

Cooking time: 40 minutes

Servings: 12

Smoke Temperature: 135Farenheit

Preferred Wood Pellet: Hard Wood Mesquite

Ingredients:

- 5 lbs. Yukon gold potatoes, large dice
- 1 1/2 sticks butter, softened
- 1 1/2 cup cream, room temperature
- Kosher salt, to taste
- White pepper, to taste
- Intolerances:
- Gluten-Free
- Egg-Free

Directions:

1. When ready to cook, set temperature to 300°F and preheat, lid closed for 15 minutes
2. Strip and dice potatoes into 1/2" cubes.
3. Place the potatoes in a foil tin and cover. Roast in the Trigger until tender (about 40 minutes).
4. Put together combine cream and butter until it dissolved.
5. Mash potatoes using a potato masher. Gradually add in cream and butter mixture, and mix using the masher. Be careful not to overwork, or the potatoes will become gluey.
6. Season with salt and pepper to taste. Enjoy!

Nutrition: Calories: 230 Fat: 2g Carbs: 45g Protein: 9g

CAST IRON SNACKS

49.   **Roasted Tomatoes**

Preparation Time: 10 Minutes

Cooking Time: 3 Hours

Servings: 2 to 4

Ingredients:

- 3 ripe Tomatoes, large
- 1 tbsp. black pepper
- 2 tbsp. Salt
- 2 tsp. Basil
- 2 tsp. of Sugar
- Oil

Directions:

1. Place a parchment paper on a baking sheet. Preheat the grill to 225F with closed lid.
2. Remove the stems from the tomatoes. Cut them into slices (1/2 inch).
3. In a bowl combine the basil, sugar, pepper, and salt. Mix well.
4. Pour oil on a plate. Dip the tomatoes (just one side) in the oil.
5. Dust each slice with the mixture.
6. Grill the tomatoes for 3 hours.
7. Serve and enjoy! (You can serve it with mozzarella pieces).

Nutrition: Calories: 40 Protein: 1g Carbs: 2g Fat: 3g

CAST IRON DESSERTS

50.   Fish Fillets with Parmesan Cheese

Preparation Time: 5 Minutes

Cooking Time: 10 to 12 Minutes

Servings: 4

Ingredients:

- 1 cup Parmesan cheese, grated
- One egg whisked
- One teaspoon garlic powder
- ½ teaspoon shallot powder
- Four white fish fillets

Directions:

1. Preheat the cast iron to 370°F (188°C).
2. In a shallow dish, put the Parmesan cheese. Mix the whisked egg, garlic powder, and shallot powder in a bowl, and stir to combine.
3. On a clean surface, season the fillets generously with salt and pepper. Dredge the fillets into the egg mixture, then roll over the cheese until thickly coated.
4. Assemble the fillets in the cast iron basket and air fry until golden brown, about 10 to 12 minutes.
5. Let the fish fillets cool for 5 minutes before serving.

Nutrition: Calories: 298 Fat: 7.8g Carbs: 5.5g Protein: 0.9g

51. Air-Fried Sardines

Preparation Time: 10 Minutes

Cooking Time: 12 Minutes

Servings: 4

Ingredients:

- 1½ pounds (680 g) sardines, rinsed and patted dry
- One tablespoon lemon juice
- One tablespoon Italian seasoning mix

Directions:

1. Warm the cast iron to 350°F (180°C).
2. In a large bowl, toss the sardines with olive oil, lemon juice, Italian seasoning mix, soy sauce, salt, and pepper. Let the sardines marinate for 30 minutes.
3. Put the marinated sardines in the cast iron basket and air fry for about 12 minutes until flaky, flipping the fish halfway through.
4. Transfer to a plate and serve hot.

Nutrition: Calories: 438 Fat: 26.3g Carbs: 3.6g Protein: 42.6g

52.   <u>Garlicky Shrimp</u>

Preparation Time: 5 Minutes

Cooking Time: 3 to 4 Minutes

Servings: 4

Ingredients:

- 1½ pounds (680 g) shrimp, shelled and deveined
- Three cloves garlic, minced
- One teaspoon smoked cayenne pepper
- ½ teaspoon ginger, freshly grated
- ½ tablespoon fresh basil leaves, chopped

Directions:

1. Warm the cast iron to 390°F (199°C).
2. Mix all the ingredients in a large bowl and toss until well incorporated. Let the shrimp sit for 30 minutes.
3. Put it in the basket and air fry for 3 to 4 minutes, or until the shrimp are opaque. Serve hot.

Nutrition: Calories: 262 Fat: 9.8g Carbs: 1.1g Protein: 3.8g